If you are politically conservative, you will probably enjoy this book. However, that may be somewhat like preaching to the choir. But, the reason this is important is that I have gathered material on several subjects of great concern that are severely testing our government's ability to even govern. Politics has trumped the common good, political correctness has paralyzed political debate and polarization has destroyed government leaders' ability to even make logical and right decisions.

Every leader is required to swear that they will protect the American citizens when taking the oath of office. Once in office, that is all out the window and we have politics as usual, which means we are short changed at best and out-right cheated at worst. The only issues that politicians can seem to be by-partisan on are pork projects (to keep themselves in office) and salary increases for themselves.

So, where does the part about 'of the people, by the people and for the people' come in? It doesn't! It has been converted, right under our noses, to 'of the politicians, by the politicians and for the politicians'. The folks don't count for anything except that we are a good resource for the funds politicians like to throw around fast and carelessly.

I am hoping that someone (younger than me) here in America, will choose to make a positive difference. They will pick up on the ideas in the book and form a grassroots movement of the so called 'silent majority' and get the ball rolling for serious government reform. I will gladly help! Newt Gingrich (www.American-Solutions.com/Platform) has made progress on this.

We must make the ideas on that website widely known. Most Americans are tired of politics as usual, most want things fixed, not patched with band-aids. I believe Americans will support people who truly want to make a real difference to better our country. Our Congress is a liability to this nation at this time.

The book takes on the dysfunctional Congress, it addresses the immigration mess, education, War on Terror, the legislation of defeat in Iraq, the gloom and doom Democrats pushing their leftist/anything goes agenda, the border fence, the turning worm, the need for just a few 'good' men and women, abortion, the audacity of the courts for becoming legislators instead of judges, and finally, the coming of a bunch of 'good' kids!

The Final Call.
Our Last Chance to Save America!

Also written by Bill Gaede … **America Has Lost It's Way … AGAIN!**

The Final Call.
Our Last Chance to Save America!

Bill Gaede

Author of America Has Lost Its Way...AGAIN!

iUniverse, Inc.
New York Lincoln Shanghai

The Final Call. Our Last Chance to Save America!

iUniverse books may be ordered through booksellers or by contacting:

iUniverse
2021 Pine Lake Road, Suite 100
Lincoln, NE 68512
www.iuniverse.com
1-800-Authors (1-800-288-4677)

Because of the dynamic nature of the Internet, any Web addresses or links contained in this book may have changed since publication and may no longer be valid.

The views expressed in this work are solely those of the author and do not necessarily reflect the views of the publisher, and the publisher hereby disclaims any responsibility for them.

ISBN: 978-0-595-48279-5 (pbk)
ISBN: 978-0-595-60366-4 (ebk)

Printed in the United States of America

In Memory of My Dad, John Carl Gaede.

"The trouble with our liberal friends is not that they are ignorant: It's just that they know so much that isn't so."

—Ronald Reagan

Contents

Foreword. xiii

Preface xv

Acknowledgments. xvii

Introduction xix

THE FINAL CALL. OUR LAST CHANCE TO SAVE AMERICA!

CHAPTER 1   P.A.D.S. 3

CHAPTER 2   Let's Roll! 10

CHAPTER 3   Fighting The War on Terror With Tied Hands! 15

CHAPTER 4   The Doom Whisperers 18

CHAPTER 5   Fence? What Fence?. 24

CHAPTER 6   For a Time Such As This. 29

CHAPTER 7   As the Worm Turns!!. .34

CHAPTER 8   Just a Few Good Men and Women 39

CHAPTER 9   America Has Murdered an Entire Country 41

CHAPTER 10   And Finally, A Bunch of Good Kids!. 43

Conclusion 47

Notes and References 49

Foreword

By way of introduction, Bill Gaede is my father, and I call him "Pops". *The Final Call. Our Last Chance to Save America* is his second book. In this episode, Pops challenges the credibility of our existing political system, but more so, challenges each of us to take control of our own futures. In addition, the book is written using his Christian beliefs, and one of these beliefs is that Christians are under attack by the vast minority! The sleeping and silent vast majority better wake up and take action.

The Final Call tackles tough issues from Iraq to immigration and from abortion to stem cell research, with just a bit of time left over for the ACLU. In reading *The Final Call* you will ask yourself:

- Why has the definition of personal responsibility and accountability changed over the years?

- Can you imagine a business ran like Congress?

- Have we become so complacent that our memories of the devastation of 911 faded all together?

- Do we want to be secure by protecting our borders, or probably worse, do we even care if we are secure or not?

The book is extremely readable and offers many ideas for repairing America, and while some folks might consider a few of them controversial, do we really think the "do-nothing" option is a viable path for moving America forward? Our government is designed by the people and for the people, but if we remain the silent majority, then by definition, the vocal minority is running our government.

My father speaks to the fundamental truth that America searches for a reason to come together, to restore national pride, and ultimately, the sense of ownership we so desperately need. Several events in our recent history prove America's ability to unite for a common goal. If it takes a tragedy to do this, maybe we should consider it a tragedy that the tail is wagging the dog.

Are the winds of change starting to blow? The book points out that some legislation is gaining ground that can reform immigration, tackle Social Security, rethink Medicare, etc. This fresh thinking is not coming from our dinosaur incumbents, but from relatively unknown freshmen to Congress. All we need are a few good men and women to be the fresh faces of change, and we have to be the good men and women that put them in office.

Pop's second book is a refreshing blend of politics and Christianity, which by the way, can work together very nicely as our Founding Fathers proved over 200 years ago. It attempts to get us off our "back sides" and work to fix what is broken. I have to admit after completing the book that I had to take a long, hard look at what I am accepting and what I am doing about it.

And finally for our Armed Forces both here and aboard, THANK YOU for your service. You are today's modern heroes. God bless you all.

Read on America and LET'S ROLL!

Jason Gaede

Plant Manager

Upstate New York

Preface

My research for this material was gathered from many reliable news magazines, articles and information from friends and family that share my disgust with our political situation. The book was written to consolidate good information and ideas for easy reading from excellent sources. And, so that people would not have to search, as I did, to find information needed to assist them in their very important political decisions! This book can serve as a valuable resource to concerned Americans.

Acknowledgments

I want to thank my wife, Sarah, for her continued patience and encouragement while I spent many hours on the computer working on the manuscript. Be blessed my love!

And my son, Jason Gaede, for writing the Foreword when he probably had too much on his plate already! God Bless!

Introduction

'The Final Call. Our Last Chance to Save America' was written out of a sense of total frustration with our government and more specifically our politicians. I want it to be published well ahead of the 2008 election, because we need to have the information available to help the folks to make their best voting decisions then and in future elections.

It is time to throw this current bunch of 'do-littles' out of office and get a fresh start. We need men and women that are willing to make the tough decisions. For the most part, this bunch currently in Congress, will not! But, we cannot stake our future on people who say it is time for a change. Sometimes, change, for change sake, can make things even worse.

We need a class of people in Congress who are not sold out to anyone and can make decisions without fear or thought of stepping on toes. To fix our current mess, someone's ox is going to get gored. It is almost unavoidable, but it must be done regardless of that ox or to whom it belongs. We need people in office who are without alliances and allegiances outside and inside of government. Politicians scratching each others backs is not working for the folks.

The change we need certainly does not come from within the government, but from outside the government. We need real change, not just a shuffling of faces from one office to another.

THE FINAL CALL. OUR LAST CHANCE TO SAVE AMERICA!

1

P.A.D.S.

That chapter title stands for Political Attention Deficiency Syndrome. In there somewhere is the state of our political system. There has clearly been an attention deficiency in our government for the last several years. It seems to get progressively worse with each election. Party does not matter much! Both are corrupt and self-serving and both are so "credit" protective, that neither is able to be effective. BUT, better to be protective than to allow the opposition party to actually accomplish something—right??

So much to write about, so little time—and—where to even begin!

We are running up to just about time for the Presidential campaign to begin. It is almost September 2007!!!! But, ugh, the campaign has already been going on for close to a year and, so far, only a couple of these ambitious candidates have dropped out! There are several others that should, but they continue to hang on for whatever reasons.

Now many of the states are moving their straw polls and primaries up to have more influence in the candidate selection! Even this is out of control. In fact, the entire process is broken and guess who is going to fix it? Politicians!! How likely is a decent fix—almost zero!

Our current crop of elected politicians seem to have no heart to "fix" anything. Many on the left seem even determined to wreck what remains that is good! The moderates that could make progress are held at bay by the left and sometimes even the conservatives. We used to be able to depend on the conservatives but they have moved toward the center/moderates, the moderates have moved left and the left has moved to the far left or in many cases, even the radical left.

I stated in my previous book, "America Has Lost It's Way—AGAIN!!", that we need to do a thorough "weeding out" of the people in both the Senate and House of Representatives. We have our first opportunity to start in November 2008. It is going to take all the folks, at home, working together to make a clean sweep and start over. We elect those people to represent us! They have zero interest in what the folks at home want and go blindly forward serving themselves.

Politicians are so dismissive of their constituents that I am angry as heck and not willing to take it anymore! Everyone should be! We MUST get up off our backsides and take our country back, before it is too late to make any difference. There is a huge abyss growing in the political and moral areas. It is getting deeper and wider. Confusion reigns!! Let all who read this know, that God is not the author of confusion.

See 1 Corinthians 4: 33

We have to win this War on Terror. We have to get our borders secured. We have to stop the raiding of all the funds that are supposed to be for Social Security! It is ALL gone, some $13 trillion is GONE and spent on Pet Pork Projects in many of our own states. Folks, those projects are not done for us, they are done for votes to keep these same scoundrels in office election after election.

We must stop the special interest groups from lobbying our politicians to vote for the things they want. (Instead of voting with the folks at home.) Then there is the wire tapping controversy, which wouldn't even be a controversy without Democrats and the mainstream media.

We should to reward good teachers and not the mediocre or worse. Have you ever seen a sport where even the worst performance gets a trophy? Of course not, what would be the point? Same question goes for teachers, why should poor teachers be rewarded as if they were good? Unions will howl, because if they lose that edge, they are not needed any longer. It is their job to maintain mediocrity and cheat our children. Unions and politicians do much the same thing these days, maintain their position, forsaking the kids and common folks! Not only do they maintain mediocrity, they promote it, just calling it some other name!

Immigration is still an out of control fiasco. There does not seem to be more than a dozen or so people in Congress that is willing to make the hard choices needed to fix this huge problem. That laborers are needed is understandable and that we are being flooded with people that are, for the most part, hard working people that want to better themselves, is also understood. What is not understandable is that no one seems to care who is coming here, what for sure, they are coming and what they are bringing with them.

We certainly know about the drugs. In fact, the government sold out two of our Border Agents, in favor of a drug peddler, even giving him immunity. He may still have immunity and is likely still hauling drugs into America. Mr. Bush continues to sit on his hands and allow these agents to be incarcerated for doing their jobs. What a shame! We don't know if there are bombs, weapons and such coming into America. But, the politicians don't care about that, they care about being re-elected and stuffing their pockets with tax payer dollars. This is unacceptable to me, I think we have every right to expect MUCH more from our elected officials.

And then there is the "FENCE", well, not really! At the current rate of progress, it "might" be finished by the turn of the century. Did I even hear that the President has asked for volunteers to help build it? You can see that he is dead serious about security!! **NOT**! At my last check, there was less than 20 miles of single layer fence complete, **zero** of the double layer that is needed to best secure the border.

Now, we are starting to get information about the North American Union—imagine European Union—for which the "Three Amigos"—President Bush, President Calderon (Mexico) and Prime Minister Martin (Canada) seem to want to build the framework. This all started in 2005, or did it start when President George H.W. Bush started talking about the New World Order? I and many others thought he was talking about the Middle East! Silly us!

But, the summit in Canada ended early, seemingly much to the delight of the Amigos, due to Hurricane Dean tearing through Mexico. And our President made light of those of us that were concerned about the meeting and their real intent!! It is safe to say, it was not a Jellybean Summit nor a Chocolate Summit as they claimed. Although, I think all three had very sticky fingers from getting them caught in the candy dish, if you get my drift.

Something else, not a word was heard from nor a question asked by any Washington politician, as far as I know, about what they were talking about at that meeting in Canada. Couldn't someone get just a little curious for goodness sake?? OR—worse—maybe they knew and just didn't care. Can you see America with no borders, no Old Glory and no control over anything! Not me! But, sources I rely on say that is exactly what they were/are trying to set up! One huge country consisting of the former Canada, former USA and former Mexico. Now—the book "The Late Great USA" is starting to come into focus! More on this in a later chapter.

And, why is Christianity the only religion on which there is a 24/7 open season. Christians are under attack like never before. It seems that Christianity is considered the most fearsome of all enemies. In recent months, upwards of 200 books have been written and published that warn of the dangers of Christianity. But, no one is concerned about Buddha, Islam, Hinduism or any of the other world name brands of religions. With the mantra of Islam being, either convert or be destroyed, we had better be paying attention. They are not a peaceful and happy group with which we can co-exist.

Anyone can criticize Christians all day, every day and not a peep is heard from the mainstream media. But, let a Koran get a drop of water on it and they go nuts! Anything even remotely connected to Christianity is fair game too, consider **Merry Christmas**, **In God We Trust** and **Under God**! More to come on this too, be assured!

I came across the following article written by a Sports Editor in Wichita Falls, Texas.

Some people, it seems, get offended way too easily.

I mean, isn't that what all this prayer hullabaloo is all about—people getting offended? At least that's what I hear the courts and the ACLU telling us. If you read Sound Off, you know I am not easily offended. Outside of getting run off the road by a Mack truck, nothing much offends me. Daddy and Mommy gave little Nicky a sense of humor.

Some people, however, weren't born with a sense of humor or they lost it in a crap game.

These people are still in the minority, but those of us in the majority are always tippy-toeing around, trying to make sure we don't step on the toes or hurt the feelings of the sense of humorless.

And you can bet there is a lawyer standing on every corner making sure we don't.

Take this prayer deal. It's absolutely ridiculous.

Some atheist goes to a high school football game, and hears a kid say a short prayer before the game and gets offended. So, he hires a lawyer and goes to court and asks somebody to pay him a whole bunch of money for all the damage done to him.

You would have thought the kid kicked him in the crotch.

Damaged by a 30-second prayer? Am I missing something here?

I don't believe in Santa Claus, but I'm not going to sue somebody for singing a Ho-Ho-Ho song in December. I don't agree with Darwin, but I didn't go out and hire a lawyer when my high school teacher taught his theory of evolution.

Life, liberty or your pursuit of happiness will not be endangered because someone says a 30-second prayer before a football game.

So what's the big deal?

It's not like somebody is up there reading the entire book of Acts. They're just talking to a God they believe in and asking Him to grant safety to the players on the field and the fans going home from the game.

"But it's a Christian prayer," some will argue.

Yes, and this is the United States of America, a country founded on Christian principles. And we are in the Bible Belt. According to our very own phone book, Christian churches outnumber all others better than 200-to-1.

So what would you expect—someone chanting Hare Krishna?

If I went to a football game in Jerusalem, I would expect to hear a Jewish prayer. If I went to a soccer game in Baghdad, I would expect to hear a Muslim prayer. If I went to a ping-pong match in China, I would expect to hear someone pray to Buddha.

And I wouldn't be offended. It wouldn't bother me one bit. When in Rome....

"But what about the atheists?" is another argument.

What about them? Nobody is asking them to be baptized. We're not going to pass the collection plate. Just humor us for 30 seconds. If that's asking too much, bring a Walkman or a pair of ear plugs. Go to the bathroom. Visit the concession stand. Call your lawyer.

Unfortunately, one or two will make that call. One or two will tell thousands what they can and cannot do. I don't think a short prayer at a football game is going to shake the world's foundations. Nor do I believe that not praying will result in more serious injuries on the field or more fatal car crashes after the game.

In fact, I am not so sure God would even be at all these games if He didn't have to be. That's just one of the down sides of omnipresence. Do you think God Almighty Himself would have watched Spearman (Texas) beat Panhandle (Texas) 50-0 Friday night if He didn't have to?

If God really liked sports, the Russians would never have won a single gold medal. New York would never play in a World Series and Deion's (Sanders) toe would be healed by now.

Christians are just sick and tired of turning the other cheek while our courts strip us of all our rights. Our parents and grandparents taught us to pray before eating, to pray before we go to sleep. Our Bible tells us to pray without ceasing.

Now a handful of people and their lawyers are telling us to cease praying.

God help us.

And if that last sentence offends you—well just sue me. (1)

The silent majority has been silent much too long. It's time we let that one or two who scream loud enough to be heard know that the vast majority doesn't care what they want. It is time the majority rules! It's time we tell them, you don't have to pray; you don't have to say the pledge of allegiance; you don't have to believe in God or attend services that honor Him. That is your right, and we will honor your right ... But by golly, you are no longer going to take our rights away. We are fighting back, **and we will win!**

God bless us one and all ... especially those who denounce Him because they need it worst of all, God bless America, in spite of all her faults. America is still the greatest nation of all.

God bless our service men who are fighting to protect our right to pray to and worship God.

2008 will be the year the silent majority is heard and we put God back as the foundation of our families and institutions. God bless our service men and women, you are the best!

On the other hand, there are those that blame America for everything that's wrong in the world! An American gets beheaded in Iraq, immediately, it is America's fault and we got what we deserved. I don't think there is a single family that has lost a loved one like that, that would agree. It is pure bunk, another innocent person got what no one deserves, and some Jihadist got another notch on the handle of his machete.

We need, as a nation of responsible people, to start to take responsibility for our own actions. What you do is not someone else's fault. The system is not unfair, you got caught and it is your debt to pay to society. Blaming things on someone else does not get it. You don't get it! And pointing to something that someone else did that may have been worse than what you did, that does not exonerate you! No matter how much you feel it should. It is still your own problem, so step up!

Choices! We make them and we must be accountable for them, regardless of how they turn out! I encourage "good" choices, rather than "easy" choices! AND, know this, many good choices are not easy.

Americans are selling out personal responsibility to the politicians! Here's what is happening. Many are deciding that it is just too much effort to take care of themselves. They have come to expect the government to do it for them. Even the obese want Congress to solve their problem and even control their kids weight. Come on! Government can't control what you eat or what you watch. It is a personal responsibility and a parental responsibility.

Even this mess about the sub prime mortgages is not a government problem. It is/was a greed problem. Mortgage companies just couldn't make enough money without cheating. They pushed mortgages onto people they knew would not be able to pay them, apparently thinking that the government would bail them out. There are some things government can do for people that lost jobs, experienced bad health, etc. But those that signed blindly are on their own.

Taxing the rich more and giving to the poor will not level the field of play. The government has used that approach for years and, is the field level? Of course not! But—we do have a nation of entitlements going for us. Some solution, huh?

So, what happens when personal dignity is sold to the politicians? Folks, they own you! But still, many people believe the guy in the pin-striped suit that says, "I am from the government and I am here to help you!"

Adam and Eve were placed in the Garden of Eden. Everything they would ever need was there in abundance. Then, Satan comes along in the form of a serpent and tricks Eve into eating of the fruit from the Tree of Knowledge, from which God had forbade them to eat. Eve immediately gave some of the forbidden fruit to Adam and he ate, at once, they realized they were naked and they hid themselves. God knew and came looking for them and called out asking, "Why did you disobey me?" Adam answered that it was that woman You gave me! Eve 'might' have suggested that it was the serpents fault! They would both be invoking the victim mentality, which is so prevalent today! Everything is someone else's fault! Folks, tain't so! **Your choices are automatically your responsibility!** <u>You</u> made them, <u>you</u> own them, <u>you</u> live with them and <u>you</u> deal with the consequences. Get used to it!

Sitting around singing "Kum Ba Yah" is not going to get the job done! It will not feed the "Bulldog" and it will not keep the foxes from the hen house!!! Come on America—LET'S ROLL!

2

Let's Roll!

The title of this chapter, is used with a great deal of reverence for the man (Todd Beamer) who said it, as well as those to whom he said it. It was perhaps only minutes before the Commercial Jet UAL Flight 93 crashed into a field near Shanksville, Pennsylvania on September 11, 2001. God Bless his family and all the other families of those that went down that day in our nation. In many ways, 09/11/2001 (World Trade Center) was even worse than 12/07/1941 (Pearl Harbor). More innocent people were lost and our <u>homeland</u> was viciously attacked. But, the anger, frustration and determination we felt was apparently soon forgotten.

That our national determination was lost, may well be in the long run, what holds the most serious consequences for America. This does not minimize the loss of life in any way, it was a horrible day. That makes it even more difficult to understand how, so quickly, we forgot. It almost seems like we have become victims to our success of preventing another attack. Complacency has replaced anger and many have wrongly decided that the attacks are over. The terrorists definitely want to attack us again—and are still doing everything they can to accomplish their goal. They will be "bock" as Governor Schwarzenegger might say!

We did stay angry long enough to go into Afghanistan and route the Taliban and al-Qaeda but we didn't stay with it and get bin Laden. We moved on to Iraq to achieve a Regime Change there, but again did not do the homework required to determine exactly what it would take to complete the task at hand!! And for sure it has been a task. Hindsight is usually good, but, it took almost 5 years to decide we couldn't do the job on the cheap. By that time, most of the folks had turned against the war effort!

The Democrats voted for it before they voted against it, the Republicans voted to support the President, even when it obviously was not working, and even that was the right vote in that situation at that time. One thing I learned from reading General Colin Powell's book, "My American Journey", is that you don't go into a war situation unprepared to win. Plan it, fund it, man it, train for it and equip it to get the job done! Then, go do it and get it over. Anything short of that is folly. Sorry Rummy! (Donald Rumsfeld, former Secretary of Defense)

FINALLY, the President has made a move that seems to be yielding results, a surge of some 30,000 troops that has made a difference in many areas and has won hearts and minds of many Iraqis that are sick of all the mayhem caused by al-Qaeda in Iraq and all the other insurgents. They have started to help the coalition forces by giving up the known locations of al-Qaeda.

Now, November 2007 as promised in September 2007, some of the surge troops are scheduled to come home, or at least out of Iraq! More are scheduled to leave bringing the total number of brigades down from 20 to about 15 and total troops to about 145,000 down from 160,000. Not over, but a good start and a promise kept.

Now, if someone will just do a surge on the Iraqi politicians and get them moving, we would really have something positive going! We need a Bill Gates or a Jack Welch or a Warren Buffett to put a team together to go there and sit with the Iraqis and get this problem hammered out. People who know that not every problem can be solved but that many can, with hard work and determination. (Many is better than the few solved to date!)

Then when that is done, come back and kick our own Congress to the side and get down to resolving problems in America! I say "some" of this in jest—but not very much! I didn't say either task would be easy, but it <u>could</u> be done by people who <u>want</u> to get it done! Our Congress is satisfied with the "do nothing" title, the "status quo", the "gotcha" mentality toward the opposite party and the "we just don't care attitude" about the folks. That is us, the folks that elected them to represent and serve us!

But—that is not even what I intended to discuss in this chapter. It does, however, segway nicely into the subject of ridding our government of the so called and 'self-designated elite' politicians, that think so much more of themselves than they ought. I believe our country would be well served by eliminating every Incumbent Senator and Representative as soon as they come up for re-election. I can't think of but, perhaps one, that is worth saving in the entire bunch! And maybe I will get into that at some point later in the book! Maybe not!

(October 24, 2007—I got word today that 33 of our Senators voted, on June 6, 2007, **AGAINST** English as America's official language!). Four of them want to be our president! Those would be Hillary Clinton, Christopher Dodd, Barack Obama and Joseph Biden.)

Those four would be a wonderful place to start in ridding the Senate of slugs! The Senator who greatly disappointed me was Joseph Lieberman. There went the 'only one' I thought might be worth saving!! So much for later in the book!

We must be unbending in our support and insistence of being an 'English only' speaking nation. Immigrants who come here must understand that and assimilate to it. If that is not acceptable, then they just need to go home.

I previously mentioned the importance of eliminating career politicians. People should be elected with the understanding that they will serve no more than 12 years, lifetime. I propose to accomplish this on a rotating basis of half the Senate being replaced every six years and the other half six years later. The House would be replaced 1/4 each four year period, with no one serving more than 12 years. In either chamber, anyone replacing a person that has not served 12 years would finish out the term of his/her **predecessor**, but also not serve more than a total of 12 years and it could likely be less. No person could serve more than 12 years, lifetime, in the House and Senate combined. Senators could not serve in the House after being in the Senate. Representatives could be elected to the Senate, but not serve more than a total of 12 years lifetime. Presidents would continue to serve no more than (2) two-four year terms, for life.

These people should be paid a competitive salary (no bonuses) with then current corporate salary structures. Health care would be purchased by the individual, to meet his/her family needs and requirements. The government would reimburse this cost up to a pre-determined limit, likely again determined from corporate group plans. These plans could be continued <u>after</u> government service at the persons <u>own</u> expense. Presidents coverage would be paid for life for him/her and spouse.

And it seems to me that expanding this idea to all the folks is dangerous. What ever we do must be done in such fashion that the government does not get into the health care business. In a country of our population, I doubt that it is even affordable. Socialized (HillaryCare nor Barackare) medicine is not the way to go. (The Congress can't even present a fiscal budget on time, how in the world would they ever manage a health care system?)

Retirement for the Senators and Representitives would be handled just as corporate retirements are, with the absolute exception of bonuses. Presidents would retire with 50% salary for a four year term or full salary for 8 year term. Retirement pay for all other elected and appointed officials would start at age 65, 67 or whatever is the widely accepted rule for the folks and at a rate of say 2% per year of service, of the average base salary achieved in their years of service. This to include cabinet members as well as other appointed positions. I believe that good people that want to make a real difference and serve their country well, would be encouraged to get involved in the political system. It would, I believe, also discourage the political parasites from even trying for office, because they would know up front that their time is limited and hopefully they would pedal their 'talents' elsewhere.

Without a doubt, current politicians will be all over this plan! Not because they like it, but because they hate it! Which would mean to me that we might be on the right track and should push forward toward implementation. Folks, this will come to pass from the grass roots, if at all. If we apply enough heat to the feet, we can get action. If we continue to be complacent with the status quo, then status quo is what we will always have. Someone once said, "If you keep doing what you have always done, you will keep getting what you have always got!" That, probably, is not good grammar, but it makes the point! [Forget that they have insulated themselves against limited terms! That, too, can be overcome!]

Now, perhaps the separate states should adopt similar guidelines for their politicians as well. If they choose to do this, it will have to come about in the same way—from the grass roots!

You say that this is just not practical. Maybe not, but the present way of doing things is certainly not working, broad and far-reaching changes need to be considered. May I remind you of our success in heading off the Scamnesty* plans of the Senate in June and again in October 2007. We can do this folks, but we have to be united, determined and unrelenting in our efforts.

* This refers to the Comprehensive Immigration act of 2007 and the Dream act of 2007, both nothing but give-away plans for illegal immigrants with an Amnesty frosting.

There are many things that Americans (not politicians) agree on even today. Newt Gingrich has done his due diligence and learned of these things. He presented it this way in a recent briefing on his web cast site:

It is time to move beyond Red vs. Blue partisan bickering and create a Red, White and Blue country. Here are some results from our surveys, which highlight the issues that Americans overwhelmingly agree on:

96% It is important for the President and Congress to address the issue of Social Security in the next few years.

95% We have an obligation to be good stewards of God's creation for future generations.

94% Children should be allowed a moment of silence to pray in school if they desire.

93% Al Qaeda poses a very serious threat for the United States.

93% In the worker visa program, each worker should take an oath to obey the United States law, and be deported if the worker commits a crime while in the United States.

93% It is important to acknowledge today, the reference to God in the Declaration of Independence—that we are endowed by our Creator with the rights to life, liberty and the pursuit of happiness.

92% Our focus should clearly be to provide long-term solutions instead of short term fixes.

91% We should dramatically increase our investment in math and science education. (1)

This is just a quick brush view of the top eight issues. The rest can be seen on the website at the end of the book in Chapter Two 'notes'.

The writers of our constitution went out of their way to establish a government for the people. Politicians have gone out of their way to re-establish the government for themselves. Remember P.A.D.S.!!??

LET'S ROLL!!!!!!!!!!!!!!!

3

Fighting The War on Terror With Tied Hands!

Much has been said about the tools we need to fight terrorism, especially by the far left and the far left leaning mainstream media. Again, this has very little if anything to do with fighting terrorism, it's all about doing anything that will hinder President Bush and disallow any progress he could possibly make. It is all politics as usual folks. And a crying shame that anyone would talk about undoing something that has served the American people well, and, yes I am talking about the wire tapping program. Let me give you some examples of how things were done back in the 50s, 60s and 70s, when Congress was controlled by the Democrats.

This from recently released, classified documents from the above mentioned period. And of course, the New York Times even tried to spin the facts around to show how the current administration is using "similar" tactics now, to fight terrorism. The real facts are that a look back at past practices used by the CIA shows how proper, legal and focused the actions being used today really are, especially in comparison. Back then, the CIA broke into houses without a warrant, wiretapped reporters in an effort to find leak sources, and even spied on Americans because of beliefs that were considered to be contrary to theirs. They even gave dangerous drugs (think LSD) to subjects without their knowledge and attempted ill advised assassination attempts against foreign leaders.

Now they are whining that the President needs a warrant to listen in on a conversation of a "known terrorist" to see what he is talking about! Now that process takes about 3 days from what I know! Hardly any of those conversations last that long. The window of opportunity is already closed before a warrant can be obtained. But, again, it is not about what is legal or needed, it is all about hampering the President in yet another way.

And of course in those days, Congress did not want to know what was being done so that they could maintain deniability. Convenient, huh? Now they want to know everything—and the safety of the public be damned. But, these activities were allowed to continue for the better part of 30 years and many were direct violations of criminal laws.

Thankfully, today these kinds of activities at the CIA are rare, if at all. (1)

Then comes the prosecutorial travesty of at least this decade, where Johnnie Sutton, the U. S. Attorney for the Western District of Texas, made his choice to become savior to a drug dealer instead of defender of Border Agents trying to do their jobs. Sure they made mistakes, what law enforcement agency doesn't, they were dealing with a criminal who resisted arrest to run back to his native land for protection and got shot in the butt. I guess it was that determination that won Sutton over to his side. Sutton gave him immunity to come back and lie about what happened. Two border agents were convicted of "obstruction of justice and assault with a deadly weapon" and even a civil rights violation! Sutton had wanted to convict them of attempted murder too! But, that charge was acquitted, they just got the sentence for it, and even more. Convicted murderers get at least 1/3 less time than the 11 or 12 year sentences dealt to the agents! And murderers don't have to be in solitary confinement! **Come on Mr Bush, wake up!** Johnnie Sutton would have been the right U.S. Attorney to be fired.

Now, here are the kickers to this travesty of justice: 1) Sutton had a choice to decide whether to prosecute a major drug dealer (he had 740+ lbs. of marijuana in his stolen van), that did not respond to law enforcement orders, or.... to prosecute border agents for shooting an escaping felon. 2) Sutton took the low road and went after the agents for trying to do their jobs. Of course you all know that they were eventually convicted and have been in prison for many months while Sutton and Bush enjoy their own freedom. 3) AND, Sutton is still Bush's friend and still has his job.

I do not know how either the President or Sutton can face themselves in the mirror each morning knowing what they have done to these men and their families. I am glad to see some semblance of a bipartisan effort to free them. At least the politicians can maybe agree, even across party lines, that this should not stand. Let's see how long it takes for justice to finally be served. And, I would hope when the next administration comes to power, that Sutton will need to seek employment elsewhere too! The President could pardon these men 'now' if he could manage to get off his hands. But, he uses his recalcitrance as if it was a virtue!

Word out today, 11/16/07, that Johnnie Sutton's favorite drug smuggler has been arrested in El Paso, Texas for charges related to his second 'load' of drugs brought to the United States in 2005. Sutton gave him immunity for the first load even in the face of him being stopped in a stolen van with 750 pounds of marijuana and resisting arrest. Osvaldo Aldrete-Davila was arrested 11/15/07 on charges stemming from the second load of drugs, while still under immunity!

One would hope this leads to the unsealing of the records sealed by Sutton, the conviction of Aldrete and the demise and hopefully conviction for Sutton. (This all sounds so much like the Duke University lacrosse case, where a "rogue county prosecutor", Mike Nifong, brought phony charges against three innocent lacrosse players.)

Finally, that Mr. Bush would 'very belatedly' do what he could have done several months ago and pardon the border agents. Maybe all this had to happen in order to 'nail' Sutton, so that justice can finally be served. I just pray for an early release for the agents and justice for Sutton.

December 2007, now comes word from grassfire.org that the President had pardoned or commuted sentences for eight drug dealers, but the agents names were still not on the list. This is unforgivable of our president and I am so bitterly disappointed that he continues to favor drug dealers over the Border Agents. What a travesty of justice! This will really look great in his legacy?

We will continue to watch this closely to see how it is handled.

4

The Doom Whisperers

Gloom, despair and agony on me. Deep dark depression, excessive misery. If it weren't for bad luck, I'd have no luck at all. Gloom, despair and agony on me! If this sounds familiar, you may have heard the Democrats, whining about just about everything. Or, maybe you heard it on Hee Haw!! Either way, read on.

This chapter is to **'honor'** those who would have us believe that all is lost if we don't listen to and follow their way of thinking. Most of these 'honors' will go to Democrats who whine and complain about absolutely everything that does not fit their own 'agenda'! Some 'honors' have to go to our adversaries who spout much the same drivel as the Democrats and a few Republicans. But, we will 'call out' our home grown champions of doom first.

I believe Senator Murtha was up to bat first with his "Let's get out of Iraq now!" chant. It was soon picked up by several others, and championed as the way to win an election! Sadly, it worked.

Then along came Senator Reid with his famous "The war is lost!", and he is staunch in his position to this day, not to be swayed by facts or good solid info from the Iraqis or our own Generals.

And not to be out-done, Senator Schumer's stupid and ridiculous "Iraq is a success in spite of the surge", and saying that "it was the inability of the American soldiers that caused the warlords to take matters into their own hands". I bet the American soldiers will be anxious to use their 'inabilities' to protect his sorry butt if/when he needs them! What a pitiful piece of work he is, is it any wonder that nothing can get done in our government with people of that caliber in power? The 'inability' of the American soldier!!!! PULEEZE!

Next we have Dick Durbin with his Dream Act for the illegal immigrants. Well, actually, it was a horrible 'nightmare' for America, that is like a cat with nine lives. It died once as part of the Comprehensive Immigration act of 2007 that was "killed" back in June 2007. Now, the Democrats and even our president are going to try to piecemeal the 'comprehensive' bill down our throats a bite at a time! First, it was attached to a defense spending bill. Then it was tweeked a little and called the Dream Act. But, it is still amnesty/scamnesty and we Americans would still get the bill for it. By the way, if you didn't catch it earlier in the news, the scamnesty bill was defeated again in October 2007.

In September 2007, along comes a Nebraska State Senator that has filed a law suit against, you won't believe it, The Almighty! He wants a permanent injunction against God! Should be interesting to see what the judge does with this one. Considering the decisions made, lately, by many judges regarding the abuse of children, more exactly their lack of concern for children and demonstrated favor toward the pedophiles, anything is possible with the suit filed by State Senator Ernie Chambers. It would be just like these 'over-reaching' judges to decide in favor of the State Senator. If so, I am thinking they might have problems with enforcement.

And of course there are John "I voted for it before I voted against it." Kerry, Nancy "We will bring honor back to the House." Pelosi, Ted "I will drink to that!" Kennedy, Hillary "We are the President." Clinton and the rest of the run away crowd. These are the people that are sworn to protect Americans, don't you feel safe now?

They seem to want to destroy the last vestiges of all that is American and put everything on the table for a great feast for every foreign person that wants to come here to the USA. And the purpose or back-ground of those coming does not seem to matter. I suppose the politicians must feel safe because of their esteemed and elevated position in America. Folks, it is time for us to remove these people from office and eliminate this political burden before they do damage that is completely irreversible! Let's clean the plate of these drudges and start fresh! We need a "draw down" from Congress, a serious re-deployment of these self proclaimed 'elites' that think so highly of themselves, send them home for good. Let's 'Return to Success' as the President said!

But—let's not ignore Dennis Kucinich, John Warner, Richard Lugar, Joseph Biden, Barak Obama, Gov. Richards, Christopher Dodd, John Edwards or Ron Paul—Huffingtons "Rock Star" of the Right! (The left wing Huffington Post-Arianna Huffington) These are the people 'leading' this country. And the really scary part is that most of them also want to be our president. God help us!! I think it is time to speak to that mountain! Matt.21: 21.

Then, there is Osama bin Laden … I don't guess he hankers to be our President, but he wants us all to convert to Islam. Now, that is just a few notches to the left of Ultra-liberal—the general direction of the liberal movement! No worries though, we must be tolerant, unless of course, it is about Christianity. Can't allow any tolerance there.

I read about an old farmer who had finally decided to buy a TV. The store installers came the next day and set it up for him, antenna and all. In the evening when he turned the TV on, all he could get was political ads, one after the other. Same thing the next morning and again that night. The next day, he called the store about the problem and they rushed right out. They checked and sure enough, nothing but political ads.

After some further checking, the repairman said he had located the problem. The antenna had been mounted on top of the windmill and it was grounded to a manure spreader. So, as politicians do, turn which ever way the wind is blowing, just like the windmill, and being grounded to a manure spreader, there was no chance, whatever, that the farmer would ever see anything except political ads.

This brings to mind the Septic Tank pumper truck in California, with the sign on the back of the truck, WARNING: THIS VEHICLE MAY BE HAULING POLITICAL PROMISES.

Now, even as General Petraeus is about to give his September 2007 assessment of the war situation in Iraq, he is being 'pre-emptively' smeared by the ultra-liberal MoveOn.org people and its supporters, the Democrats. The Democrats are actively supporting MoveOn and the DailyKos. They are afraid to stand up to them, lest they be smeared in similar fashion. These are the spineless people that want to be our President, and still they have the nerve to talk about leadership! We are clueless in Washington.

On September 15, 2007, there was a war protest in Washington. This demonstrates what I am talking about, for the common folks to get something done, we have to be that passionate about it, and organized! As far as these protesters are concerned, I rank them right up there with Reid and Schumer! I probably should have said right 'down' there, where the gutter snipes hide!

Now, there is a new group called Gathering of Eagles! They were organized in 2007, by **veterans**, to challenge war protesters! How refreshing is that? Rep. Duncan Hunter even paid a surprise visit to the Eagles during the protest and told the protesters that it is for 'this' generation that we will win the war on terror. 'This' generation is the one that appears bent on the demise of America as we know it. And, **yet**, our brave men and women in uniform fight on, to preserve the right to act stupid and irresponsible in this country.

Here, I am reminded of an email I received a while back. It stated that there have been only two men, all throughout history, that have offered to die for the freedom of others. **Those were Jesus Christ and the American Soldier.** Thank you Jesus and God Bless **ALL** American service men and women!

Think about this:

It appears we have appointed our worst generals to command forces, and our most gifted and brilliant to edit newspapers. In fact, I have discovered by reading newspapers that these editor/geniuses plainly saw all my strategic defects from the start, yet failed to inform me until it was too late.

Accordingly, I am readily willing to yield my command to these obviously superior intellects, and I will, in turn, do my best for the Cause by writing editorials—after the fact.

~~Robert E. Lee 1863~~

"Congressmen who willfully take actions during wartime that damage morale, and undermine the military are saboteurs and should be arrested, exiled or hanged."

~~President Abraham Lincoln~~

Works for me!!

This should remind you of earlier paragraphs in this chapter and specifically statements made by the likes of Murtha, Schumer, Reid, Clinton, Paul and Lugar. This kind of rhetoric is irresponsible, stupid and serves no good purpose for America.

It seems appropriate here, to mention a politician who recently was doing a photo-op in a classroom of second graders.

On the subject of blood circulation, he was trying to make the matter clearer, saying, "Class, if I stood on my head, my blood would run into it and I would turn red in the face." "Yes," the class said. He then said, "Why is it that while I am standing upright, in the usual manner, the blood does not run into my feet?"

A little fellow in the back of the room shouted, "Cause your feet ain't empty!"

From NewsMax.com

Not nearly enough fuss has been made about the MoveOn character assassination ad about General Petraeus. Every right thinking American, especially those in position to get in front of a TV camera or on a talk show should shake this like a dog shakes a snake—until it is dead. Tell them you are going to remind them of their venomous ad, then remind them of it and then tell them what you reminded them about, ad infinitum.

What a despicable organization and what a shame that the Democrats are so spineless and fearful of it. These are the people that campaign about offering fresh leadership. They have exactly nothing to offer. Leadership is about tough choices and not one of the MoveOn supporters/sympathizers even approaches that level of ability.

David Limbaugh says he is amazed that the ongoing debate over the war skirts the real question that should drive all our decisions. We are focused on the hardships and costs of staying the course, but rarely, if ever, discuss the consequences of abandoning it.

Even when the President based his plan on the Generals testimony of drawing down the troops to pre-surge levels by next summer, the Democrats immediately came against that too. (1)

This is General Petraus, the general that the Senate confirmed, unanimously!

And I totally agree with Limbaugh, it is insane to not be discussing the consequences of abandoning the War on Terror in Iraq. The terrorists won't go away if we walk away!

I am confident, that if the President gave the order to immediately cease all operations in Iraq, the Democrats would cry foul again, they have not even a shred of a plan for "what then"!

Then comes the proposition of: **What If MoveOn.org Existed 65 Years Ago?**

Envision a picture of General Eisenhower, 5-Star General.

And under his picture, the following:

GENERAL EISENHOWER OR
GENERAL LIES AND POWER?

Cooking the Books for the White House!

General Eisenhower is a man constantly at war with the facts. He believes that Nazi Germany is a direct threat to the United States. It was Japan who attacked us, not Nazi Germany.

Most importantly, General Eisenhower will not admit what everyone knows: America is in an un-winnable war on two fronts that are thousands of miles away. Even if America could win, we could have to keep thousands of troops in Europe for decades.

General Eisenhower has become General Lies and Power for not retreating and sending our troops home.

Source unknown.   September 2007

Now if that doesn't create an instant requirement to run to the bathroom and heave, you need to read it again—more slowly. Are you feeling safer now, knowing that about half the Presidential candidates are supporters of MoveOn.org?

Regardless of where you stand on the issue of the US involvement in Iraq, here's a sobering statistic for your consideration: There has been a monthly average of 150-160 thousand troops in Iraq for several months now. The firearm death rate calculates to about 60 (ugh) per 100 thousand soldiers per month, if all the statistics are close.

The firearm death rate in Washington D.C. stands at about 80.6 per 100 thousand people for a similar period. So—you are 25% more likely to be shot and killed in the nations capitol than in Iraq! (2)

Maybe we should pull out of Washington!! Do us all a favor Congress, "CUT AND RUN".

If you can still find comfort in those statistics, consider that D.C is currently ranked number 19 on the 2007 list of Most Dangerous Cities in America! (2)

5

Fence? What Fence?

Can't you just hear a very indignant and sarcastic John Wayne saying, "'What the hell do you mean—dial "1" for English?'" I can just about imagine him reaching right through that phone and grabbing someone by the throat!

Well, that is why we need a John Wayne right now! To reach into the DHS (Department of Homeland Security) and grab someone by the throat, until the fence is complete. All 854 miles of it! That's where border security starts, but we know the Bush administration is not about security, he is about no borders at all, north or south. Now, he has the support of the Kennedy Democrats and small Democratic majorities in both chambers to help him shove it all down our throats. Where are you Big John?

That's probably why no one was in Congress was asking questions when the President was in Canada in August 2007 with his 'Amigos' from Mexico and Canada. They (Congress) surely had to know what was being discussed and just laid low! That way, they can always say—we didn't know! Deniability is a wonderful thing in politics! Character and integrity are apparently only for the folks back home! They are to be treated like mushrooms: Feed 'em crap and keep them in the dark.

Now, we get back to Dr. Jerome Corsi's book, "The Late Great USA", and we learn that as early as June 2005, Robert A. Pastor, a **North American Union** advocate, testified to the US Senate and advised of his plan for building a North American Community consisting of Canada, Mexico and the USA. His report offered, <u>to the Senate</u>, a blueprint of the goals that the three countries of North America should pursue and the steps needed to achieve these goals!

Now, I understand why Congress did not say a word nor ask a question regarding what the 'Three Amigos' were talking about in Canada during the great JELLY BEAN conference!! <u>They knew and were complicit</u>!! What leadership we enjoy in Congress! And yet, they have the nerve to criticize Iraqi government officials!

I came across an article said to be written by Sebastian Vilar Rodrigez, most likely from Barcelona, Spain. I have been unsuccessful in efforts to confirm that Rodrigez is even a real person or that the 'article' was even published in a newspaper or magazine. I think the name is likely a pen name used to protect from almost certain attacks from Muslims.

He titled it "ALL EUROPEAN LIFE DIED IN AUSCHWITZ" and it reads as follows:

I walked down the street in Barcelona, and suddenly discovered a terrible truth—Europe died in Auschwitz. We killed six million Jews and replaced them with 20 million Muslims. In Auschwitz we burned a culture, thought, creativity, talent. We destroyed the chosen people, truly chosen, because they produced great and wonderful people who changed the world.

The contribution of this people is felt in all areas of life: science, art, international trade and above all, as the conscience of the world. These people were burned.

And under the pretense of tolerance and because we wanted to prove to ourselves that we were cured of the disease of racism, we opened our gates to 20 million Muslims, who brought us stupidity and ignorance, crime and poverty, due to an unwillingness to work and support their families with pride.

They have turned our beautiful Spanish cities into the third world, drowning in filth and crime.

Shut up in their apartments they receive free from the government, they plan the murder and destruction of their native hosts.

And thus, in our misery, we have exchanged culture for fanatical hatred, creative skill for destructive skill and intelligence for backwardness and superstition. We have exchanged the pursuit of peace of the Jews of Europe and their talent for hoping for a better future for their children, their determined clinging to life because life is holy, for those who pursue death, for people consumed by their desire for death for themselves and others, for our children and theirs.

What a terrible mistake was made by Europe. (1)

Regardless of the source of these words, the truth within can hardly be denied.

If this is starting to sound familiar, you have probably been doing your homework. If not, it is about time for you to start. This in no way is completely related to the Mexican people coming here in droves. But in many ways it is, for instance the parts about crime, poverty—likely our own—because we can't continue to pay for the birth of all the anchor babies born here every day—all the medical care and medication for those that need it—for social security for those that never paid a dime into the fund—for all the destruction and debris they leave behind on their illegal trek into our country—for the damages done to crops and livestock—and on and on.

Thank God, most of them do come here to work, they do work and try to feed and house their families for the most part. Most of the Mexicans will assimilate in a few years if **WE** make the rules. The ones that don't assimilate, will be in prison or back to their native land, but that is only if we make and enforce the rules. The #1 rule is that America is an English only, speaking country. The #2 rule is that if you don't like rule #1, leave. This is simple enough for everyone.

But, an ever increasing number of Muslims are also coming to this country. We have no clue how many have entered America from the south. We have no idea where they are or what was their purpose for coming here. Of equal concern, are those in America (mostly politicians and ultra-liberals) who do not seem to care that many are here to plan our demise and destruction. These are as dangerous to America as the terrorists and maybe in some ways more dangerous.

They may or may not be planning our destruction, but are complicit in that they are enablers of it. And, of course we do have some home grown terrorists that have come to hate America as well. These types would likely be misfits anywhere they live, but they will stay in America and spew their venom, because of our freedoms. They can get by with it here, in many other countries, they would just be shot—problem resolved.

But, getting back to the fence—which is progressing at the blinding speed of a land slug, nothing can really improve with regard to immigration until the border is secured. This is why we must listen carefully to the presidential candidates with regard to their solution for securing the borders, or lack of it. If we don't cast our votes for the pro-security candidate, we are doomed. This next election, Nov. '08 may well be our last chance to have a president that will secure our borders, and he will need the support of many in the House AND the Senate that will support that position with their votes. And, likely, they will need to vote for security again and again because the Democrats seem to be bent on turning the USA over to legal and illegal immigrants. It might be a strategy that will keep them in power, but in a very few years, there will be little left to have power over. So their point is—??

And now this from Grassfire.org 12/12/2007

Today, Jerome Corsi of WorldNet Daily has posted a story regarding the Hutchison (Senator Kay Bailey[R]-TX) amendment to the Department of Homeland Security (DHS) appropriations bill.

In the article, congressional staffers confirm that the amendment does, in fact, give DHS discretion over the location of the fence. Even more, DHS would not be required to build the double-layer fence mandated by the Secure Fence Act nor required to even build a fence at all.

Go here to read the article:

http://www.wnd.com/index.php?fa=PAGE.view&pageid=45018

The plain fact is that Congress passed a law that mandated a double-layer fence covering 854 miles of our southern border. That is what the American people reasonably expected to happen when the Secure Fence Act was passed and signed into law last year.

But the Hutchison amendment has the real potential to essentially gut the Secure Fence Act.

Senator Hutchison and others who supported her amendment **did** vote for the Secure Fence Act. They may sincerely support border security and may have good motives for wanting to give DHS discretion. But this amendment creates a loophole that means the double-layer fence mandated by the Secure Fence Act is no longer mandated and final decisions are left up to DHS on if and where the fence is built.

As a staffer for Rep. Duncan Hunter said, quoted in the WorldNet Daily article, "This new requirement no longer mandates that fencing be double layered."

Time Line of Events Surrounding Fence Act Hoax

+ 9/29/06, prior to vote—Sen. Bill Frist sends strongly worded letter to House And Senate leaders setting out the plan to pass subsequent legislation gutting the Secure Fence act.

+ 9/29/06, 9:30 PM—Secure Fence Act passes.

+ 9/29/06, late evening—Hutchison makes comments from the floor asking for discretion on implementation of Secure Fence Act; and submits the Frist letter into record.

+ 9/29/06, 1–2 hours later—DHS appropriations bill passed with discretionary funding for border security not specifically tied to the Secure Fence Act

DHS questions necessity of border fence

It gets worse, the funding bill passed by Congress required that DHS report to Congress on how it would spend the funds prior to most of the funds being released. It is in the DHS's report that it becomes clear that neither Congress nor the Administration really ever intended on adhering to the Secure Fence Act. First, DHS's plan—called SBInet (Secure Borders Initiative)—does not reference the goals of the Secure Fence Act, Second, DHS's report back to Congress in December 2006 openly questioned whether the border fence was necessary.

Instead, DHS arbitrarily decided there should be 570 miles of total border barriers, of which 370 miles would be actual pedestrian fencing. Thus, instead of 854 miles of double-layer fencing, DHS set a goal of 370 miles of "pedestrian" fencing (i.e. not double-layer fencing). It is clear that DHS felt no obligation to fulfill the specific requirements of the Secure Fence Act.

But that's just the beginning …,

Border Fence Scam of 2007

Skip ahead to this past fall as Congress has been considering a $3 billion funding bill for border security and allegedly the fence. As you may know, that amendment was stripped out of the Department of Defense appropriations bill last week. But even if they had passed the $3 billion funding amendment, DHS will not be required to use any of that money for the border fence! Not ONE DIME!

That's because of another amendment put forward by Senator Hutchison that said DHS would not have to build the fence. The amendment (SA 3176), seems at first glance, to support building a fence. It is entitled "Improvement of Barrier At Border". (2)

Sen. Hutchison's amendment and the $3 billion were subsequently dropped from the DOD appropriations bill. However, the amendment was concurrently attached to both the DHS and DOD appropriations bills, just as the Senate leaders promised. There is little chance that the grassroots folks, that's us, can kill this amendment before the end of the Congressional session. I will report on it if time permits!

Our Congress is now living out a pack of lies and trying desperately to hide their lies from us, with regard to their real intent of border security. So, if they lie about this, they will lie about anything else! God help us!

6

For a Time Such As This

It is a pitiful situation that our 'best hope' seems to be that those in power seem to implode every few years. They get so self righteous and greedy, that they start to think that they are above the law and infallible. It is about then that things start coming to the surface and the wheels start to fall off. Witness the Dan Rostenkowski mess a few years back, the demise of Tom Delay, the Abramoff fiasco and all those that fell as a result of unbridled greed. The Congressman that had $80,000 in his freezer and is still serving in Congress, will he ever be convicted? (Nov. 2007, I read he has finally been indicted!!)

Then there are the pedophiles that go for congressional aids through the Internet and who knows what other ways, a Senator that solicits sex in a Minneapolis restroom, and even a past President that tinkered with a young intern, and got by with it. I am sorry folks, but I expect more than this from the people we elect. They are supposed to serve the folks and America, not themselves.

Great Scott, do I need to go further? Is there any doubt that we need to clean house of these people and have a fresh start. Congress complains constantly about the fact, and it is a fact, that the Iraqi government has not made much progress in the last 12-14 months. But, what has our Congress done in the same period of time, darned near nothing.

At least the Iraqis have made progress in five of the benchmark areas. When the Democrats swept into power in 2007, they were going to complete many items of urgency in the first 100 days. It has been 8 months now (240 days approximately) and as far as I know, they got the minimum wage bill passed and the implementation of the rest of the 9/11 Commission Recommendations. (most were already implemented) Those are mostly good things, but that's all folks!! Oh, and they did, very reluctantly, fund the war on terror—for a while. And still they have the unmitigated gall to criticize the Iraqis!

Hey, I am sick of the war too! But, we must support the troops to complete the job. If they don't finish it there, we will likely have to finish it here. And that will be a lot more costly in blood and resources than doing it now. Folks, diplomacy does not work with these Jihadists, they want us either dead or converted to Islam—maybe both. Then America can be a economic waste-land like Iran, Iraq, Syria, Egypt, etc. Sure, they are making 'progress' in some of those countries, but their standard of life is eons from ours. They desperately want their standard for us!

In a time such as this, God was sorry He had created man on the earth. Gen. 6:6

I can understand if He is having those kinds of thoughts again in this time. And, I am not just referring to the murderous radical Islamists. There is plenty for Godly disappointment going on right here in America, by Americans. We claim to be about 85% believers in God, but our lack of action would suggest 1: We either don't really believe, or 2: We feel like the government should take care of us, or 3: we are just complacent, lazy and apathetic!

I am telling you that our politicians are not for us folks! They are only interested in themselves. If you are not getting this now, perhaps you need to go back and read chapters three and four again, very carefully. I do not mean to be condescending about this, but everyone needs to understand that ours is no longer a government of, by and for the people.

Let us hear the conclusion of the whole matter: Fear God and keep His commandments, For this is man's all. For God will bring every work into judgment, Including every secret thing, Whether good or evil. [In case that sounds familiar, it is the last two verses of Ecclesiastes.] NKJV

So, if you are not yet convinced, not to worry, it gets worse. When it is all said and done.... a lot more is being said than done. But, I believe that the best of America is yet to be seen.

Think about this!

"Evil is powerless if the good are unafraid!" Ronald Reagan said that!

I certainly do not think America is afraid, but there are plenty of organizations out there that would like us to be, and to hide under our desks as Bill O'Reilly says. The ACLU comes to mind. They would like us to think every thought and action that is in the least bit Christ-like is to be shunned and hidden from the public. Radical Islamists would have us in fear of offending them or their Koran or Allah. Far left liberals will tolerate everything imaginable.... except things Christian or even things hinting of Christianity. They attack everything from 'Merry Christmas' to 'In God We Trust' on our currency! And yet they will defend Islam to the death.... ours.

Folks, I am at the point that I am not much worried about offending the ACLU, nor the far left, the Atheists nor even the Muslims. Christians worth their salt know that Christians will be offended often. It says so in the Bible (see Matt.18: 7), so we need to get used to it, develop a thick hide and make ourselves a respected presence in this nation. I am talking about in the voting booth, in the streets, in the media, both print and the air waves. There are 80 or more of us and only 10—15 of them!! It is time for us to stop the tail from wagging the dog.

Right now, 11/11/07, there is an ongoing effort in Congress to silence opposition views, those being mostly Christian. These acts are cleverly disguised as if they are protecting people from hate crimes. The real intent is to silence the pulpit from even 'saying' that it is against Gods teachings to be gay or lesbian. Any effort from the right (read Christian) to be heard or to disagree with the ultra liberal agenda, would be out of bounds or reason. The intent is to silence anyone disagreeing with, their anything goes, agenda. They, the Democrats also would like to reinstate the 'Fairness Act'. There is nothing fair about it, it is hoped that the 'act' will stifle the conservative talk programs. They say it is just not fair that the radical left leaning talk shows can't compete even when propped up by people like George Soros and his billions.

I want to relate a personal story to you to illustrate the point that Americans can come together, without a horrific incident such as 9/11. My wife and I were on the way to Alabama for the 2007 Thanksgiving holiday, traveling south on Interstate 85. We were approaching the South Carolina/Georgia state line and traffic was moving very well. Just then, my wife said, "Oh oh, the brake lights are coming on up the road." As I looked in the distance, a huge cloud of dust shot up 75 feet, maybe more, into the air and I commented that that wasn't good!

We were all soon totally stopped, we were almost to the bridge over the river that divides the two states. At the Georgia end of the bridge, about one hundred yards ahead of us, there were 3 cars and an 18 wheeler tangled in a bad accident. Soon, there were fire trucks, ambulances and helicopters arriving from all directions. The Jaws-of-life soon were at work trying to free the folks from one flattened car. Some people were pressing closer to see, the police officers finally taped the area off like a crime scene and they even formed a human shield around the car as the injured were removed. I guess it was just too much for most people to even see.

As we walked on the bridge toward the accident, people were talking as if they knew each other. There did not seem to be a stranger in the bunch. Nor was there a complaint to be heard, even though peoples plans had been seriously hampered for that day. Everyone seemed to be focused on those injured, some were praying, a college student from Clemson was thanking God that his class did not let out earlier for the holiday, because, even a few seconds could have placed him at the point of the accident. A delivery man from 84 Lumber had been delayed a few minutes earlier, otherwise, he too could have been in the accident and it was the same for us. There was no sign of prejudice, everyone was on the same page, people of all races, colors and creeds were relating and talking together. There was a man with a very well trained black Lab. Retriever that entertained us for a few minutes with a number of tricks his dog did.

Was it not for the tragedy, this could have been a huge 'tailgate' occasion, one stretching for 15-20 miles before traffic got moving again, some 4 hours later. For sure, there was not any party spirit, but one of thanksgiving because most were spared, and of coming together, because we are, after all, all God's people. It gave assimilation a whole new meaning.

This was a huge tragedy to some, perhaps many, however by comparison to 9/11, it was not close to the same. It was a huge tragedy for those that were injured, or worse, and their families. It was a huge tragedy to the young man on his way to his grandmother's funeral. He would have turned off I-85 at the very next exit past the bridge. He never made it, I doubt he was even able to get to his destination in time to be at the cemetery for her burial. I hope he did. The last 84 Lumber delivery did not get made that day.

I said all that to say that Americans just need a good reason to come together as a cohesive force. It doesn't have to be a 9/11 and it doesn't even have to be a tragedy, I believe we are all searching for something to grasp upon that will improve lives, make us safer and re-instill the spirit of pride in this country. A new president won't do it! We will still have the same squabbling, power hungry, ineffective and self-serving politicians in Congress! But, there is a small group of politicians that may be different, more on that in the next chapter.

We must search out those people who 'really' want to make a difference for this country. We must encourage them to run for office and back them 100% and throw the bums out that are currently in power. Now that seems to me to be something we could all get behind and support just like what occurred after that automobile accident!

Can we do that?

Albert Einstein put it this way: The world is a dangerous place to live, not because of the people who are evil, but because of the people who don't do anything about it.

It goes without saying that most of the politicians aren't doing much about it. The Republicans seem too timid to really take on the Democrats. The Democrats are so "hate filled" and self-invested, that they won't allow anything to get done for fear of being smeared as a Bush sympathizer or supporter. Both parties are too self-centered to actually represent the folks that voted them into office.

On the other hand there are a number of great organizations that are really working hard to turn things in the right direction for this nation. I hesitate to name them, because I don't want to leave anyone out where I am aware of their good efforts. Having said that and in no particular order, here goes anyway: NumbersUSA, Fire Society, Liberty Counsel, Freedom Works, Kim Clement Ministries, Grass-fire, ACLJ, American Solutions, Newsmax Media, Fox News Channel, American Family Association and maybe even the Blue Dog Democrats. I know there are many more that I am not that familiar with, but check these sources out for a reasonable view and in my belief, a truthful viewpoint.

7

As the Worm Turns!!

Is is just me or are we starting to see a change in the wind direction? And maybe, just maybe, it even started as far back as 2004 when Senator Tom Daschle (D), a liberal Senator from South Dakota, was defeated by a relative newcomer, John Thune (R).

Check out these recent events:

In recent weeks, more so than before, there have been several important issues that have gone the way of the conservative view. The big one of course is the turn around in the war on terror in Iraq, much of that brought about by added troops and a new plan, maybe just as importantly, the Iraqis finally got full "up to here" with all the violence, mostly against each other and started cooperating with the Americans. They 'ratted' out the insurgents hide outs, ammo stashes and bomb making facilities. The Troops cleaned the bad guys out and stayed there to make sure they did not return. They destroyed their safe houses and bomb facilities. As the Iraqis saw this working they told the troops even more, etc., etc. Places considered 'lost' a few months ago are now thriving and people are playing ball, doing business and relaxing where before they were afraid to even leave their homes. There are many other very positive things happening in Iraq now, that were impossible even in the spring of 2007.

Dispatches from Iraq, 11/16/07, Christians come back home! Michael Yon is an independent journalist and former Green Beret. He was embedded in Iraq for several months in 2005 and returned this year to continue reporting on the war. A snippet of his recent dispatch is as follows:

Yesterday a bishop came to St. John's Church in Baghdad and was welcomed by the local folks. There was a service held by the Most Rev. Shlemon Warduni, at the church. It was attended by soldiers from the 2-12 Infantry Battalion, who were instrumental in securing the streets of this neighborhood, members of the

Iraqi Army 3rd Div. also involved and the local folks that were delighted to welcome the Christians 'home'! (1)

And also, high up on the list of important issues is immigration reform. NOT THE DREAM ACT, BUT <u>REAL</u> REFORM. Reform like the American folks have been screaming for over the last 2-3 years. It is known as the **Secure America with Verification and Enforcement (SAVE) Act.** It was introduced by the Chairman of the Immigration Reform Caucus, Rep. Brian Bilbray (R-CA) and my former Rep. Heath Shuler (D-NC). (I have recently moved from his district) Keep H.R. 4088 in mind, it is even bi-partisan if you can imagine such a thing. Congressman Shuler is a member of the Blue Dog Democrat Coalition, which seems to have a whole new approach to governing! Their information is worth looking up on the Internet!

The SAVE act emphasizes a serious e-verification program requiring Fed. agencies, employers and contractors to verify the eligibility of all employees in a 1—4 year span, depending on their number of employees. All the departments and government agencies will be able to share info on SSNs (Social Security Numbers) and thus duplicate SSNs will be eliminated. Border security will be strengthened by adding 8,000 agents to the Border Patrol and expand investigative abilities if Immigration and Customs Enforcement. Cong. Tom Tancredo has signed on, I hear, as well as Rep. Duncan Hunter, both advocates of border security.

There are already other supporters signing on as well, like NumbersUSA, a <u>very</u> critical link in preventing the Scamnesty Plan and Dream Act from becoming law, in 2007. I am saddened to say that President Bush would have signed either one of these pitiful bills, had they been passed by congress. But, the folks rebelled at the thought and the politicians folded, at least enough to stop these travesties.

And now, only a few days after I first read about the SAVE act, it is picking up major support in the way of The National Federation of Independent Business (NFIB) which represents more that 600,000 small businesses in every state. This has to be embarrassing to big business, when small businesses show their willingness to put an end to hiring illegal immigrants!

And then, just a day later, I read that Senators are falling all over one another to be first to sponsor the bill in the Senate. How political of them, they did "the very best they could" according to Senator Spector, just a few months ago when they came up with the Scamnesty Plan. Now they are scrambling to jump on a bill, written in part, and sponsored by a freshman congressman. That sure confirms to me, that we need more fresh thinking in Congress.

Also, The International Brotherhood of Electrical Workers (IBEW) has come on board in support of the SAVE act with its 752,000 worker members.

These endorsements are big, folks. Let's support the bill and all its co-sponsors!

11/29/07 Another promising house bill from a thoughtful young congressman, Rep. Jeff Flake, (R) Arizona, is the SMART act. (Secure Medicare and Retirement for Tomorrow) Congressman Flake came to Congress in 2001.

The SMART act tackles two of the most important challenges facing America and Americans. 1) replacing the flawed pay-as-you-go Social Security system, and 2) simplifying Medicare and allowing consumers to manage their own health care. It transitions over 42 years so as not to shock the current system and does not affect those already in those programs.

Basically, every persons' name is on 'their' own Social Security and Medicare contributions such that Congress can't rip it off and spend it on 'pork'! (They prefer the term 'earmarks' now!) Their individual funds can then be invested, by them, in 5 different mutual funds and ensures that all workers will have access to affordable health care even <u>after</u> retirement. It is believed that this new solution will be very attractive to young workers and hopefully we will be hearing much more about this bill soon. Remember H.R. 4181. (2)

Suffice it to say, at this point, that the A C L J (American Center for Law and Justice) has become and is a major thorn in the side of the ACLU (American Civil Liberties Union). The ACLU is anything but a civil liberties organization and certainly does nothing to protect the kids, the Bible, the Christians nor the rights of American citizens. But, they are all about protecting the pedophiles, keeping the Ten Commandments off government property, taking "In God We Trust" off our currency, promoting the gay agenda in our schools and eliminating "Under God" from the Pledge. That's the kind of things they are about!

There are many areas where the ACLJ has been very active and successful, in protecting rights and freedoms and by thwarting illegal policies against Bible reading in schools, etc. I have not been permitted to share them with you in detail, but, the ACLJ needs to be recognized for their many good efforts in any case. (3)

Liberty Counsel is a defender of Christmas and CHRISTmas as well as Christmas trees! They should never to be called Holiday trees, says Liberty.

I say if that offends 10—15%, the whiners, who cares!!? The real effort ought to spent on 'not' offending the other 85% of the folks. This year, 2007, Christmas is back in most stores! Maybe the rest will finally 'get it' by next Christmas.

Liberty prints lists of the stores that are the biggest offenders of all.

Last year, Best Buy and Eddie Bauer were at the top of the 'naughty' list. Let's see what they do this year, 2007. Wal-Mart has returned to Christmas after causing a huge uproar in 2006. Old Navy and The Gap are apparently still hold-outs!

Liberty Counsel intervened on behalf of a local resident in West Bend, WI after a library director would not allow a flier about the annual Life Chain event to be posted. After receiving a FAX from Liberty Counsel, he had a sudden change of heart and the flier was posted on both library bulletin boards.

Just before Thanksgiving, Liberty Counsel sent a strongly worded memo to the Fort Collins, Colorado city council regarding their proposed action to ban red and green lights, as well as religious displays, explaining that it would be a clear violation of the Constitution. And what a surprise, the proposal was influenced by an ACLU "volunteer". The good news is that the city council voted overwhelmingly to reject the proposal.(4)

Additionally, Liberty Counsel has had about 45 other victories during 2007 in the areas of: Religious Freedom, Sanctity of Human Life and Traditional Family values. This according to their year end report. see:

www.libertyaction.org/10181/2007YearEnd.htm

And just today, 11/13/07, I learned that a man unknown to politics and to Indianapolis, Indiana residents a few short weeks ago, has been elected the cities' new mayor. The folks were ready for a change and since he was unknown in politics, <u>maybe he could be trusted</u>. And many also reported being more **against** the Incombent than **for** the challenger, but the combination was enough to dislodge a sitting mayor! Now, this is what I am talking about, clear the political slate and start with new people that want to make a difference. Perhaps Rep. Heath Shuler (D) falls into that category, we sure hope so in Western North Carolina. Also, Rep. Jeff Flake (R)—Arizona.

Now this: 11/26/07 A Japanese scientist, announces his discovery of an embryo-free way to produce genetically matched stem cells. Now, every scientist, whether concerned about destruction of embryos or not, can and will embrace this new technique. It is said to be simple, powerful and non-destructive. This brings "the great stem cell debate" to its conclusion. (5)

President Bush has fought this morally corrupt procedure since mid-2001. Now, he is finally vindicated for his stance.

Visualize a huge ocean-liner, out in the middle of a vast ocean, starting to make a turn to return to port (read common sense) and ever so slowly, it is entering the turn. The straight wake behind the ship (read business as usual) is starting to show a bit of a curve (read change) and maybe, just maybe, we are about to see positive things starting to occur on a regular basis.

I am thinking and praying that we will see more and more good and right things occurring as we move forward. I am excited and hopeful. No irrational exuberance just yet though!

8

Just a Few Good Men and Women

This chapter is to be a complete reversal of the things and people mentioned in Chapter 4, The Doom Whisperers. This is what our government could look like with all new faces. Good men and women that want to make a real difference, do right, effective and good things that strengthen America and improve life. There are some 300 million people in America now, perhaps 205 million (1) voting eligible people. So, if we need 513,000 (1) to re-elect all the political offices in the country, that is a very small percentage of the folks. Soooo, we really do need just a few good men and women to put all new people in office. That (513,000) is just 1/4 of 1% of those old enough to serve.

"A democracy is always temporary in nature; it simply cannot exist as a permanent form of government."

"A democracy will continue to exist up until the time the voters discover they can vote themselves generous gifts from the public treasury."

"From that moment on, the majority always vote for the candidates who promise the most benefits from the public treasury, with the result that every democracy will finally collapse due to loose fiscal policy, which is always followed by a dictatorship."

"The average age of the worlds greatest civilizations from the beginning of history, has been 200 years."

"During those 200 years, those nations always progressed through the following sequence: from bondage to spiritual faith; from Faith to courage and from courage to liberty; from liberty to abundance; from abundance to complacency; from complacency to apathy; from apathy to dependence and from dependency back into bondage."

Author is unknown.

Folks, this is what is at stake. Apathy is the greatest danger to our freedom! After apathy is dependency and then finally, bondage.

If the average of 200 years survival time for a Democracy is even close to right, we are already living on borrowed time. Two hundred years was up in 1987!!!

And now, this just in: The difference between Republicans and Democrats!

A Republican and a Democrat were walking down the street together and they came upon a homeless person. The Republican gave the homeless person a business card and told him to come to his office for a job. Then, he reached into his pocket and handed the person a $20 bill.

The Democrat was quite impressed by this and shortly they came upon another homeless person a few yards further. The Democrat decided he would help this person and gave him directions to the closest welfare office. He then reached into the Republicans pocket, took $20, gave the homeless person $5 and kept $15 for administrative fees.

Now, you know the difference!

Seriously folks, we haven't yet fought the good fight. We haven't finished the race, but we must not quit. We must keep the faith!

In one of Winston Churchill's most famous speeches, during the second world war, he told his battle weary troops, "Never, never, never give up!" They didn't and we must not either. To give in or give up now would be to snatch defeat from the jaws of victory. Know this—Christians are Victors—not Victims. We cannot, we must not and we will not fail!

9

America Has Murdered an Entire Country

Since January 22, 1973, the date Roe v. Wade was finalized into law by the Supreme Court, we have been complicit in the destruction of about 50,000,000 (that's **million**) American babies. This is the equivalent of a 'small' country! These babies represent almost 17% of our current total national population, or almost one in five. If you put all the people in the United States into circles of 5 people in each circle, you could say that the sixth person is missing from almost every circle. That is our murder rate in addition to that which is recorded, an additional and astounding 1,470,588 per year.

Folks, 50 million is equivalent, in population, to a country almost 1 1/2 times that of Canada, more than twice that of Romania and almost 8 times that of Israel. So, it is not difficult to show that we have murdered an entire country.

This year, 2007, every one of the Democratic candidates running for the nomination for president have said that they would appoint Supreme Court Justices that would sustain Roe v. Wade. If one of these people should be elected, there are some scary statistics just around the corner relating to mass murder of children. And yet, presidents and presidential candidates 'swear' to protect the people of America.

The Republican candidates seem to have a variety of opinions:

Giuliani—thinks the ultimate decision should be left up to the women, not the government. But—he says he will appoint judges that might be expected to rule against abortion.

Romney—changed his mind a couple years ago (2005) from supporting choice to being pro-life. In a speech in 3/2007 he said, "It is the people who are sovereign in America, not a few folks in black robes, Judges add or take away from the constitution." He says, now, he would protect life.

Thompson—says he would appoint judges likely to support outlawing abortion. It is his goal to see Roe v. Wade overturned, then he said, "Sometimes states have a right to do things that even Fred Thompson disagrees with!"

Huckabee—disagrees with Thompson regarding states rights on abortion. He says, "If morality is the point here and if it is right or wrong, not just a political question, then you can't have 50 different versions of what is right or wrong!" "For those of us who think this is a moral question, you simply can't have 50 different versions of what is right!" said Huckabee.

McCain—Seems to have a pro-family voting record. Now, he's trying to mend fences, destroyed in 2000, with conservative Christian activists. And speaking of fences—his stance on immigration has hurt him bad! He is done! Hang up the spurs! But—as we have seen with Mike Huckabee and Barack Obama, a lot can change in a few weeks! (And, it certainly did!)

God is about to use the children of the United States, that have survived Roe v. Wade, to confound the government and return the common sense, so long absent from politics and politicians.

Consider these recent prophesies:

This nation was born to be a Christian nation and God said, "I'm bringing you back to what your forefather's prophesied, this is eternal and it will happen". 3/11/07

Abortion was legalized, but the children that survived will raise up and become a force in this nation. Churches will be purged out and cleaned and become a place to be proud of. 2/23/07

Your children are mine says the Lord. I will take them and cause them to prophesy to the governments and to the principalities! 3/4/07

God said this is the year of the child and the woman. 3/11/07

The children are waiting to hear the sound of the Father whispering in their ears, 'I Love You'. There remains a Father's heart in this nation. The Spirit of Elijah is about to come upon this holy nation. 6/17/07

There is a burden that God carries for this nation. It has been chosen by God to bring forth a new fantastic move of the Spirit that will reach the unreachable and touch the untouchable. 3/17/07

These are excerpts from prophesies spoken as dated, by Kim Clement. In the first excerpt, God declares that America was born to be a Christian nation. He promises to bring it back to that reality. In the last excerpt, He basically reconfirms that the work He has begun, will be completed. I guess the ones in between describe His helpers.

10

And Finally, A Bunch of Good Kids!

Since January 22, 1973, we have destroyed a country of kids. Today, the oldest of these kids would have been about 34 years old and all those born before January 1990 would be voters. There would have been an additional 1.5 million new voters each year. But, in the infinite wisdom of those then in Congress and the Judges in black robes, it was decided to kill them.

But, getting back to the title of this chapter, where do 'good kids' come from? Easy answer, good parents! So where do good parents come from? Now, I have quit writing and started meddling, huh?

Where do 'good' teachers come into play? Good teachers are very instrumental in the development of kids. So, they come into play starting at ages 4-5 or even earlier in some cases. Regardless of when teachers come in, they play a tremendous roll in kids lives and also what kind of parents these kids will become in their own child rearing years.

Going back to chapter one, I mentioned that good teachers should be recognized and rewarded for their positive influence on their charges. By rewarded, I do mean financially rewarded. These teachers are so valuable to our children and our nation that we have short-changed them for years. And in doing so, we have short-changed our kids as well. Folks, these are our kids and they are our future, we will depend on their education to run this nation in the future.

There was recently an after dinner discussion, around the table, just talking about life.

One man, a big shot in the community apparently, decided to explain the problem with our education system. And, it had nothing to do with No Child Left Behind! His argument had to do with <u>all</u> children being left behind. He said,

"What is a kid going to learn from someone who decided his/her best option in life was to become a teacher?"

He reminded the other folks at the table what they say about teachers: "Those who can, do. Those who can't, teach!"

To stress his point, he said to another person, a young woman, "You are a teacher, Natalia, be honest, what do you make?"

Now Natalia had a reputation for honesty, integrity and being straight forward said, "You want to know what I make?" After a short pause, she looked directly at the big shot and started:

"Well, I make kids work harder than they ever thought they could.

I make kids sit through 40 minutes of class time when their parents can't get them to sit 5 minutes without an I Pod, a Game Boy or a movie.

I make kids feel like a C+ is a Congressional Medal of Honor.

You know what else I make?

I make kids wonder.

I make them question.

I make them apologize and mean it.

I make them have respect and take responsibility for all their actions.

I teach them to write and then I make them write. A keyboard may not always be available.

I make them read and read and read some more.

I make them show all their math work. They use their God-given abilities, not a man made calculator.

I make my class room a place where all my students feel safe.

I make my students stand, placing their hand over their heart to say the Pledge of Allegiance to the Flag, One Nation Under God, because we live in the United States of America.

Finally, I make them understand that if they use the gifts they were given, work hard and follow their hearts, they can succeed in life."

After a brief pause, Natalia continued:

"Then, when people try to judge me by what I make, with me knowing money isn't everything, I can hold my head high and pay no attention because I know they are ignorant … You want to know what I make?

I MAKE A DIFFERENCE! What do you make **Sir**??"

Author unknown.

Now, that's what I am talking about, that is a TEACHER!

Teachers are our first line of defense when it comes to the critical development years. Teachers are an extension of parents, they deserve parental respect, support and involvement. They are NOT replacement parents, stand-in parents or responsible for your kids. That is called parenting and taking responsibility as a parent. Teachers are responsible to 'teach' kids, not raise them.

So, why is our education system in such a shambles? The short answer is 'politicians' and the correct answer is 'politicians'. My final answer is: POLITICIANS! Well, I should give the far left liberals some of the credit. After all, they have worked hard to destroy our education system, and all the while getting considerable assistance from politicians. Back in the day, there used to be states-men and states-women in Congress. Those were called the good old days, remember?

Thank God for our good teachers and for the good kids they send out into this nation. Thank God for caring and responsible parents. It does not take a village to raise a kid, it takes a Mom and a Dad in the best of worlds. Make no mistake, many good kids come from single parent homes. Given viable options, I believe most parents would agree that they are both vital to parenting success. I don't really consider that two Moms or two Dads are a viable option. There is still much to be learned about this new parenting concept! It will be interesting to see if this concept becomes self perpetuating from generation to generation in the same way that welfare has.

THE END

Conclusion

It is my hope that you will, after reading the book, come to at least similar, conclusions as the ones I have proposed. We must win the war on terror. We must turn our government around such that it is people driven again. We must start that process now and start by methodically rebuilding Congress with new people, who are from the folks and beholden to no one.

We can no longer sit by while the 'elites', as they like to think of themselves, use our government for their own benefit. We must return the government to the people. We must eliminate career politicians and put them out of government for good.

We need a regime change from top to bottom. We need people in government that want to 'serve' America and Americans. We have seen way too much already of those that are self-serving and greedy.

We have seen enough of people like the Apostle Paul describes in his first letter to Timothy. "He is proud, knowing nothing, but is obsessed with disputes and arguments over words, from which come envy, strife, reviling, evil suspicions, useless wranglings of men of corrupt minds and destitute of the truth, who suppose that godliness is a means of gain. From such withdraw yourself." 1 Timothy 6: 4 NKJV

I have recently been impressed by some of the relatively new congressmen though. Rep. Heath Shuler (D) North Carolina, has co-sponsored the SAVE act, Secure America with Verification and Enforcement, a new and thoughtful approach to the issue of immigration reform.

Also, Rep. Jeff Flake (R) Arizona is co-sponsoring the SMART act, Secure Medicare and Retirement for Tomorrow. Bottom line, every persons name would be on his/her own Social Security and Medicare accounts. That will prevent the politicians from raiding the funds for their pet projects and squandering them as they have some $13 trillion they have already ripped off from the folks.

I am just learning about the Blue Dog Coalition and those folks seem to be of the quality I am suggesting. Hopefully, they will not be changed by the career politicians that they have to rub shoulders with each day.

This is what I am talking about! New people with fresh new ideas and right ways of thinking. People interested in making a difference that will actually improve lives, secure our borders and increase our safety and secure a future for Americans. People willing to step-up and take action for 'the greater good'.

Notes and References

Chapter 2

(1) Nick Gholson,   "Taking Offense at Prayer? God Help us!",
Times Record News, Wichita Falls, TX   1999.

(2) Newt Gingrich, "Weekly Solution: America's Red, White and Blue Plat-
form",
AmericanSolutions.com,   November 8, 2007.

Chapter 3

(1) Ronald Kessler,   "CIA Secrets Reveal Wisdom of Bush Policies",
NewsMax,   September 2007.

Chapter 4

(1) David Limbaugh,   "Democrats Won't Budge on Successes in Iraq"
NewsMax.com,   September 14, 2007.

(2) Infoplease.com,   "Safest and Most Dangerous Cities", 2007.

Chapter 5

(1) Sebastian Vilar Rodrigez,   All European Life Died In Auschwitz",
Publisher uncertain,   November 21, 2004.

(2) Grassfire.org Alliance,   "The Fix is In: Congress Guts Secure Fence Act",
From the desk of Steve Elliot,   December 12, 2007.

Also, see Special Report: "Government Border Fence Trickery"
FireSociety.com,   November 13, 2007.

Chapter 7

(1) Michael Yon,   "Dispatches From Iraq: Come Home",
FoxNews.com,   November 16, 2007.

(2) Dick Armey,   "A Smart Approach to Retirement Security",
FreedomWorks.com   November 13, 2007.

(3) Jay Sekulow, ACLJ,   American Center for Law and Justice.

(4) Mathew Staver,   Chairman-Liberty Counsel,
Search Liberty Counsel site,   2007.

(5) Shinya Yamanaka, search by his name,   November 2007.

Chapter 8

(1) Newt Gingrich,   www.AmericanSolutions.com   2007.

Chapter 9

(1) Kim Clement,   www.kimclement.com   2007.

978-0-595-48279-5
0-595-48279-1